JOSH McDOWELL

Skeptics Who Demanded a Verdict

POCKET GUIDES™

Tyndale House Publishers

Pocket Guide is a trademark of Tyndale House Publishers, Inc.
Library of Congress Catalog Card Number 89-50818
ISBN 0-8423-5925-7
Copyright ©1989 by Josh McDowell
All rights reserved

Printed in the United States of America

02 01 00 99
12 11 10 9 8 7

CONTENTS

The Skeptics' Quest

The New Testament describes salvation—
the way one is made right with God—as
coming in a variety of ways:

- "He who stands firm to the end will
  be saved" (Matthew 10:22, NIV).
- "Whoever acknowledges me before
  men, I will also acknowledge him
  before my Father in heaven"
  (Matthew 10:32, NIV).
- "If anyone would come after me, he
  must deny himself and take up his
  cross and follow me" (Mark 8:34,
  NIV).
- "Sell everything you have and give to
  the poor. . . . Then come, follow me"
  (Mark 10:21, NIV).
- After Zacchaeus made restitution,
  Jesus said, "Today salvation has
  come to this house" (Luke 19:9, NIV).
- "Whoever lives and believes in me
  [that Jesus is the Christ, the Son of
  God] will never die" (John 11:26, 27,
  NIV).
- "Repent and be baptized" (Acts 2:38,
  NIV).

- "Believe . . . and . . . love one another" (1 John 3:23, NIV).

These descriptions do not represent disparate formulas for salvation; rather, they enumerate some of the barriers that keep individuals from faith.

Some people are stumped by the intellectual obstacles to accepting the fact that Jesus is the Christ, the Son of God. They must surmount that skepticism and come to a point of belief.

Some struggle with confessing their sin. They must repent. And the authenticity of repentance is sometimes well demonstrated by restitution.

Some are too shy or prideful to tell anyone. They must become bold enough to admit their faith to others. Public baptism is the primary, biblically prescribed way.

Some people worship other gods—themselves, their backgrounds, their possessions. They must renounce all such idols. Denying themselves, leaving home, selling their possessions are the radical steps necessary to make Jesus Lord.

Most of us are such three-dimensional people that all these factors must be addressed to some degree as we come to faith. But usually there is one area that stands out as our primary hurdle. That is why Scripture records Jesus addressing individuals according to their personal barriers—"repent," "believe," "forsake all," "confess," "be baptized," "love one another."

This book is about three people who were skeptics. For them, intellectual belief was the great blockade. They could not easily believe that Jesus was who He said He was. But they were also honest—honest enough to demand a verdict. Jesus promised: "Ask and it will be given to you, seek and you will find; knock and the door will be opened to you. For everyone who asks receives; and he who seeks finds; and to him who knocks, the door will be opened" (Matthew 7:7).

God more than fulfilled that promise to these men. For instance, once C. S. Lewis, who counted himself an atheist, committed himself to a quest for the truth, he found that God would not leave him alone. New information kept coming to Lewis's attention so relentlessly that he felt as though he were in a great chess match in which his "Adversary" kept making "moves" that finally brought him to a point of "checkmate." The process recalls what the Apostle Paul said about the Thessalonians: "From the beginning God chose you to be saved through the sanctifying work of the Spirit and through belief in the truth" (2 Thessalonians 2:13).

If you are equally committed to following the truth to wherever it leads, you will enjoy the story of these three men who did the same.

Charles W. Colson served as special

counsel to President Richard M. Nixon from 1969 to 1973. During the Watergate investigation Colson was indicted on a charge unrelated to Watergate. Oddly enough, the panic and breakdown of the Watergate cover-up provided him with compelling evidence for the validity of the resurrection of Jesus Christ and the truth of Christianity.

C. S. Lewis was the renowned author and professor of medieval and Renaissance literature at Magdalene College, Cambridge University, from 1954 to 1963. Following the death of his mother in his childhood, he became a committed atheist. It was not until he was "checkmated" by his "Adversary" that he became "surprised by joy," a joy he had longed for all his life.

Josh McDowell was an eager university student looking for meaning in life. He was skeptical about religion. But some friends challenged him to examine the claims that Jesus Christ is God's Son, that He took on human flesh, that He lived among real men and women and died on the cross for the sins of mankind, that He was buried and arose three days later, and that He could change a person's life in the twentieth century. McDowell didn't think there were facts to support those claims. But then he started to investigate. . . .

Charles W. Colson

CHARLES W. COLSON is a native of Boston and holds degrees from Brown University and George Washington Law School. From 1969 to 1973 he served as special counsel to President Richard M. Nixon. During the Watergate investigation Colson was indicted on a charge unrelated to Watergate. He had nothing to do with either the planning of or the cover-up of the Watergate break-in but felt compelled to admit his wrongdoing in a related break-in—the burglary of psychiatrist Daniel Ellsberg's office. He was indicted for smearing the name of Ellsberg (which the administration had claimed had been necessary on the grounds of national security) and served seven months in prison.

Rather than hardening him, Colson's time in prison gave him a greater love for people. Following his conversion to Christianity, not only did old political enemies become friends, but while in prison new friendships were forged with those who might have become enemies.

Presently, Colson is chairman of Prison Fellowship, a ministry he founded in 1976, which makes its headquarters in Washington, D.C. He is also the author of Born Again, Life Sentence, Loving God, *and the recently released* Kingdoms in Conflict. *Here is his story, told in his own words, as taken from* Loving God, ©1983 Zondervan Publishing House, *and from* Born Again, ©1976 Fleming H. Revell Company.

Saturday, June 17, 1972, was warm and oppressively humid, typical of summer in Washington, D.C. As special counsel to the president of the United States, I was on call day and night, leaving little time for myself or my family. But this Saturday we were enjoying a rare, uninterrupted family day at our suburban McLean, Virginia, home.

Patty and the kids were stretched out by the pool, and I was starting up the grill for a cookout, when the phone with the direct line to the White House switchboard rang. It was John Ehrlichman, one of the president's senior assistants. Without explanation he brusquely asked what seemed like a ridiculous question: "Where is your friend Howard Hunt?"

Hunt was a shadowy ex-CIA agent I'd known casually and had recommended for a minor White House job investigating leaks of government documents. But it had been months since I'd seen him or heard from him. So I pressed Ehrlichman.

What in the world was so important about Howard Hunt's whereabouts as to interrupt my quiet Saturday afternoon?

It was then I learned for the first time that a group of ex-Cuban freedom fighters had been arrested while breaking into the Democratic National Committee offices in the Watergate hotel. One of the men had had a piece of paper in his pocket with Hunt's name on it. I can still remember my distracted thoughts as I hung up the phone: *Hunt's no amateur. He wouldn't get involved in a common burglary. Yet if he had been . . . I know him . . . my name could be dragged in.*

Then I shrugged and dismissed these foreboding thoughts, went back to the pool and steamy sunshine, and grilled some hamburgers.

That was how Watergate began for me.

WHAT THE WATERGATE
SCANDAL SHOWED ME
During the following weeks I was comforted by my belief that no one in the White House or the Nixon campaign would be so stupid as to think they could find anything of value at the headquarters of a bankrupt party being ignored by its own candidates. This was no moral judgment, just practical politics. Even as the burglars' connection to Howard Hunt and his compatriot G. Gordon Liddy was un-

covered, it was dismissed; both men had been part-time White House consultants but had been removed from the rolls months earlier.

Though the break-in was a burglary under D.C. law, it seemed at the time to be nothing more than campaign spying to me—like stealing the signals out of the other team's huddle. Certainly it was nothing much more than things I had done or others had done to me in my twenty years of political campaigns. (It was not until two years later, in the summer of 1974, when the infamous "smoking gun" tape was released, that the world as well as some of us on the inside learned that in the early days after the break-in the president was involved in attempting to sidetrack the FBI's investigation. That would later become *the* cover-up.)

In light of what happened later it sounds naive, but at the time I believed nothing more was at stake than surviving the political brick-throwing through the November elections. The whole affair would then be neatly buried beneath the electoral landslide, and we would get on with the more important business of governing the country—or so I thought.

In the post-election euphoria that November, no one paid much attention to Watergate. I recall only occasional discussions about it with the president, who was consumed with the frustrating negotiations to end the war in Vietnam. Henry Kissinger was shuttling back and forth to the Paris peace talks. But Haldeman, chief of staff, and John Ehrlichman were busy reorganizing the bureaucracy for the second term. John Mitchell, former attorney general and campaign manager, had moved back to his lucrative law firm in New York. And I was packing up my office preparing to return to my own Washington law practice.

Then in January of 1973 Watergate, at least from my perspective, began to take on new implications. Howard Hunt, fearing imprisonment, sent his lawyer to see me. As the attorney demanded assurance of clemency for Hunt (which I refused to give him), I learned for the first time that the Watergate burglars were being given funds for support and legal fees.

Following the visit of Hunt's lawyer, I consulted my law partner, Dave Shapiro, a two-fisted trial veteran who had scrapped his way up from the streets of Brooklyn. Together we broke out the law books. It was then, late in January 1973, as we reviewed the tight columns of fine print in the criminal statutes, that I began to understand the possible criminal implication for the White House.

So in mid-February, with the Vietnam War finally over, I summoned up the courage to confront the president. It was during our last meeting in the Oval Office before I returned to my private law practice that I gave President Nixon the painful advice: "Whoever did order Watergate, let it out . . . let's get rid of it now. Take our losses."

The president had been leaning back in his chair, legs crossed and feet propped up on his massive mahogany desk. The words were barely out of my mouth when he dropped his feet and came straight up in his chair. "Well, who do you think did this? . . . Mitchell? Magruder?" He was angry, righteously so, I supposed, that I would suggest putting the finger on a loyal aide. He was also, I still believe today, oblivious of the possible criminal implications, even as the net was being drawn increasingly tighter around us all.

THE COVER-UP BEGINS

According to the exhaustive records compiled from tape recordings, mountains of documents, endless congressional hearings, and massive volumes of testimony, the first serious Oval Office discussion of likely criminal involvement took place the morning of March 21, 1973; that was the fateful meeting when John Dean warned the president of the "cancer on his presidency."

Later on March 21 (the specific dates are important), Haldeman called Mitchell in New York, and Mitchell, in turn, told

Jeb Magruder, his campaign assistant, he would "assist" him if he went to jail. That was also the day $75,000 in additional money was dispatched to Hunt for "lawyer's fees." The president conferred again with Haldeman and Ehrlichman and Dean. And that same evening the president, without disclosing anything that had gone on that busy day, called me at home for a thirty-one-minute conversation.

Though I had officially left his staff, it was not surprising to receive a call from the president; he had told me he wanted to continue to call on me for advice. What was surprising was the president's impatient, almost distracted voice. I had spent countless hours across a desk from him or on the phone and could almost always read his mood. When big issues were on his mind, like Vietnam bombings or dealings with China, the president was remarkably cool. When little things came to his attention, like sniping in the press, he seemed the most unnerved.

The evening of March 21 he quickly dispensed with small talk and plunged into Watergate.

"What's your judgment as to what . . . what ought to be done now . . . whether, uh, there should be, uh, a, uh, report made or something, you know, or just hunker down and take it or what?"

The official transcripts show my reply. "The problem I foresee in this is not what has happened so far—that is, the mystery

16

of the Watergate. I don't know whether somebody else higher up in the Committee for the Re-election is gonna get named or not but, uh, to me that isn't of any great consequence to the country if it happens. The thing that worries me is that, is the possibility of somebody, uh, charging an obstruction of justice problem—in other words, that the subsequent actions would worry me more than anything."

I then went on to suggest that the president remove Dean and appoint an independent special counsel to handle Watergate for him. Though I wasn't aware then of earlier meetings with Dean and the others, it was, as hindsight confirms, good advice. But those chilling words "obstruction of justice" must have made the president's day. No wonder he didn't call me again for two weeks.

After March 21 everything changed—it was all downhill, and fast. Conversations grew thick and heavy the next week: talk of perjury, "stonewalling," obstruction of justice, the kind of stuff that gives grown men weak knees and sweaty palms.

On March 23 Judge Sirica released a letter from one of the Watergate burglars who had made a deal; he would tell all in exchange for a lighter sentence. That afternoon Haldeman called me with a series of questions: Had I promised clemency to Howard Hunt? Had I urged the campaign people to get intelligence on the Democrats? Bob's voice was cool, as always, but from the way he repeated my answers, I was certain someone else was in the room with him—the president. His questions also revealed what was happening behind the massive iron gates of 1600 Pennsylvania Avenue. The occupants were stocking the bunkers for what they now realized would be a bloody siege. Increasingly distrustful of my colleagues and sensing that all was not well, I dictated a memorandum of our conversation as soon as I hung up the phone.

PANIC SPREADS

Thinly disguised panic began to sweep the plush offices of the stately old building that houses the most influential and powerful men in the world. Events escalated so fast that there was no way to keep track of them. As the press bantered allegations that campaign officials had ordered the break-in, Dean rushed off to Camp David to write a "report."

On March 26 the grand jury reconvened to hear new charges from one of the original burglars. That same day Dean called Magruder and taped his conversation.

On March 27 Haldeman and Ehrlichman discussed the crisis for two and a half hours with the president. Also, Mitchell met with Magruder to discuss clemency, while Mitchell's wife, Martha, made one of her legendary calls to the *New York Times,* charging that someone was trying to make a "goat" of her husband.

While at Camp David on March 27, John Dean had secretly contacted an old law school classmate for advice on the best criminal lawyer he could hire. Five days later he retained a tough ex-Kennedy administration prosecutor, Charles Schaeffer. Then on April 8, 1973, Dean met with Watergate prosecutors to bargain his testimony for immunity and save his own hide, as he acknowledged with refreshing candor in his memoirs.

Within hours the cover-up collapsed. Magruder, already in contact with the prosecutors, began negotiations in earnest. Dave Shapiro, sensing it was now "every man for himself," coaxed me into taking a lie detector test to establish my innocence, then gave the results to the *New York Times.* The prosecutors called me; I offered to testify.

The White House was like a frontline command post under heavy shelling. Though men like Ehrlichman and Haldeman put on a brave front, they trusted no one and were taping every phone conversation.

Daily headlines fed the public fresh tidbits, mostly from stories leaked by aides or their lawyers seeking to clear their skirts or entice the prosecutors into a better deal. Meanwhile, the prosecutors were so busy with White House officials offering testimony that they couldn't handle the traffic in and out of their offices. Suddenly Watergate was a three-ring circus.

History reveals that after the criminal investigation of the White House began—as it did with Dean's April 8 meeting with the prosecutors—the end of Mr. Nixon's presidency was only a matter of time. The cover-up was discovered—and doomed—and this is why the dates are so important. For though the cover-up technically dated back to the June 1972 break-in, the serious cover-up—the part everyone knew or should have known was criminal—really began March 21, 1973. And it ended April 8, 1973.

BY NATURE,
CONSPIRACIES COLLAPSE

With the most powerful office in the world at stake, a small band of handpicked loyalists—no more than ten of us—could not hold a conspiracy together for more than two weeks.

Think of what was at stake: Each of us involved—Ehrlichman, Haldeman, Mitchell, and the rest—believed passionately in President Nixon. To enter government service for him we had sacrificed very lucrative private law practices and other endeavors; we had sacrificed our family lives and privacy; we had invested our whole lives in the work, twenty-four hours a day if necessary. Only a few months earlier the president had been re-elected in a historic landslide victory; the ugly Asian war was finally over; we were riding the crest in every way.

Think of the power at our fingertips: A mere command from one of us could mobilize generals and cabinet officers, even armies; we could hire or fire personnel and manage billions in agency budgets.

Think of the privileges: A call to the military aide's office would produce a limousine or jet airplane; the National Gallery delivered classic paintings to adorn our office walls; red-jacketed stewards stood in waiting to serve food and drink twenty-four hours a day; private phones appeared wherever we traveled; secret service men were always within sight—as many as we wanted.

Yet even the prospect of jeopardizing the president we'd worked so hard to elect, of losing the prestige, power, and personal luxury of our offices was not enough incentive to make this group of men contain a lie. Nor, as I reflect today, was the pressure really all that great; at that point there had certainly been moral failures, criminal violations, even perjury by some. There was certain to be keen embarrassment; at the worst, some might go to prison, though that possibility was by no means certain. But no one was in grave danger; *no one's life was at stake.*

Yet after just a few weeks the naturally human instinct for self-preservation was so overwhelming that the conspirators, one by one, deserted their leader, walked away from their cause, and turned their backs on the power, prestige, and privileges.

THE IMPLICATIONS FOR CHRIST'S RESURRECTION

So what does all this have to do with resurrection of Jesus Christ and Christianity? Simply this: First, God used the tragedy of Watergate to bring me to faith in the resurrected Christ. Watergate revealed how fleeting power and prestige were, and how meaningless they could be in the face of personal loss. Power and prestige had been what I sought, yet they left me personally unfulfilled and both personally and professionally exhausted. I came to find out that Jesus Christ offered what power and prestige never could.

Second, Watergate offered an excellent historical example that, oddly enough, provides compelling evidence for the validity of the resurrection of Jesus Christ and the truth of Christianity. I would like to look at this a little more closely, beginning with my personal experience and then tracing the parallels between the Watergate scandal and the Resurrection.

NO RELIGIOUS INTEREST

While growing up, I had never really been a religious person. All my life had been spent trying to find personal and material security, trying to be a success in all that I did. I grew up in America in the Great Depression years. I recall how terrible it was for people to stand in bread lines, people without enough food to eat. I was the grandson of immigrants, and came from a family that had never sent anyone to college. I remember thinking, if I could just get a scholarship to college, that would be security. I'd find meaning, purpose in life, that's all I'd need.

So I earned a scholarship to an Ivy League university and graduated with academic honors. But I found that wasn't enough. I was then commissioned as an officer in the Marine Corps during the Korean War. I remember pinning those bars on as a marine lieutenant, hoping that would be my identity.

After the war, I earned my law degree and became the youngest administrative assistant in the United States Senate. And I can remember working my way up that ladder thinking: *I am going to find security; I am going to find meaning; I'm going to find purpose out of the things of this world.*

When I was just thirty-nine, the president of the United States asked me to come and to work with him. I was given an office right down the hall. The White

House and politics are just like the business community. The closer you are to the president, the more powerful your position, and soon I had an office immediately next to the president.

One day I remember looking out over the south lawn of the White House, those beautifully manicured grounds, and thinking to myself, *My dad used to tell me in the depression that if you work hard and strive to get ahead you can do anything in America.* I remember thinking, *That's right, it's true. All those years I wanted that security, I wanted success and power and achievement, and now I've got it all.*

SUCCESS LIKE SOAP BUBBLES— BEAUTIFUL UNTIL GRASPED

But the amazing paradox: When I left the White House (choosing to go back into private practice shortly after President Nixon's second inauguration—before, really, the darkest days of Watergate and before I thought I was in trouble myself), I walked out with really everything a person could want in life, but I felt absolutely empty, dead, and hollow inside. All those things I thought would give me security and meaning, did not.

I then returned to what was now a very prestigious and lucrative law firm that I had helped found. Upon my return, clients were lining up at the doors, the result of a rash of articles like the feature piece in the *New York Times* describing me as "the first bona fide member of the president's inner circle—well on his way to becoming one of the busiest and best paid lawyers in Washington." *All of this—the warm welcome, plenty of money—surely,* I thought, *this will give me a new thrust.*

A few short weeks after my return to law practice I was in New York to meet with the producers of a promising TV system which might in time give the networks tough competition. We met in the offices of one of New York's old-line investment banking houses. Soon the company's president, chairman of the board, three vice-presidents, and two bankers were seated around a long boardroom table, peppering my associate with facts, figures, statistics, and information about their plans for multimillion-dollar investments. My associate was eagerly taking notes. I could not. For the first time in my life I was not able to concentrate in a meeting; it was all I could do to appear interested, nodding, I hoped, at the right times.

Am I having a blackout? I asked myself. Something serious must be wrong with me physically; I can't still be tired. Once I imagined that someone had drawn a soundproof glass window right across the table, leaving the mouths on the other side moving soundlessly. Finally, the meeting was over. We closed the deal, a healthy six-figure amount, and they flew us home in their corporate jet.

On the return trip I settled back into my plush seat of the private Gulfstream II and tried to shut out the world. I stared out the window, alone again with the same doubts and worries that had been my un-welcome companions for five months. In the old days, landing a big account was ex-hilarating—reason to take Patty to dinner to celebrate. *Where is the old competitive zest?* I asked myself. I finally concluded that the decompression from the tension-packed White House years to law practice was an adjustment that simply would take time, although time did not seem to be solving the problem.

CHANGE IN AN OLD FRIEND

There was one client I'd represented before whose return I welcomed: the Raytheon Company, an electronics manufacturer and the largest employer in New England. I was again to be their general counsel. In mid-March I flew to Boston for all-day meetings with the company's top executives. The executive vice-president, Brainerd Holmes, who once headed the government's manned-space program, was an old friend. His boss, Tom Phillips, the company's president, had climbed to the top by sheer wits and raw ability.

I met Brainerd first in the company's modern brick and glass headquarters overlooking Route 128, the busy beltway around Boston. Holmes, enthusiastic about Raytheon's new programs, scheduled me for several meetings with engineers and vice-presidents. Later in the day Tom Phillips left word that he, too, wanted to see me before I departed.

As I started for the president's office, Brainerd stopped me. "Chuck, maybe there's something I should tell you about Tom before you go in there. He's had quite a change—some kind of a religious experience." Brainerd paused, searching for the right words to explain it. "I don't really understand it, but it is quite important to him. He—he might come on—well, you know, maybe a little strong." Brainerd concluded with an embarrassed smile.

This was surprising news. Tom Phillips had always been such an aggressive businessman; it was hard for me to see him teaching Sunday school. I thought that was for little old ladies. Once he'd told me he was Congregational in the same way I labeled myself Episcopalian. Nothing important—just another membership. I thought that he might be involved in church fund-raising, as the top executive of the state's biggest company would be expected to do for church and community.

When I entered his office, he was the same old Tom, jet-black hair, athletic build, stripped down to shirt sleeves, as always. But the smile was a lot warmer, radiant, in fact, and he looked more relaxed than I had ever seen him.

"Tell me about yourself, Chuck. How have you been doing?" he began.

An honest answer would have been that I felt rotten, but Tom was an important client, so I told him, "I feel fine, a little tired."

"You really should get some rest, Chuck. It's important after what you've been through," he said, and I had the curious sensation that rather than making small talk, he genuinely meant it.

We reminisced about old times, then it was back to me. "About this Watergate business, Chuck, are you okay? It looks to me like people are trying to drag you into it."

I told Tom I had no direct or indirect involvement in the burglary—despite the heat from the press. I was launching into a lengthy defensive explanation when Tom cut me off. "Don't explain. If you tell me you weren't responsible, that's all I need to hear."

TELL ME ABOUT IT
We had talked for twenty minutes, and nothing at all had been said about religion.

Yet Tom *was* different. There was a new compassion in his eyes and a gentleness in his voice. "Uh—Brainerd tells me that you have become very involved in some religious activities," I said at last.

"Yes, that's true, Chuck. I have accepted Jesus Christ. I have committed my life to Him, and it has been the most marvelous experience of my whole life."

My expression must have revealed my shock. I struggled for safe ground. "Uh, maybe sometime you and I can discuss that, Tom." If I hadn't restrained myself I would have blurted out, "What are you talking about? Jesus Christ lived two thousand years ago, a great moral leader, of course, and doubtless divinely inspired. But why would anyone 'accept' Him or 'commit one's life' to Him as if He were around today?"

The conversation turned to more comfortable subjects, and then Tom walked me to the door of his office, his long arm around my shoulder. "I'd like to tell you the whole story someday, Chuck. I had gotten to the point where I didn't think my life was worth anything. Now everything is changed—attitude, values, the whole bit."

Phillips was boggling my mind. "Life wasn't worth anything," he'd said. When you're president of the biggest company in the state, have a beautiful home, a Mercedes, a great family, probably a quarter million-a-year salary . . .

THE EMPTY LIFE

But he had struck a raw nerve—the empty life. It was what I was living with, though I couldn't admit that to Tom. I went back to Washington to struggle with my inner malaise—and Watergate—and Phillips' astonishing words.

Following my time with Tom came what I've called "the long hot summer." During the summer of 1973 the story about the Nixon tapes broke, the television hearings with the Ervin committee reached a crescendo, tempers were flaring, and political morality had been reduced in Washington to the level of bayonet warfare. Being personally attacked both in print and on the air, and being falsely accused of smearing a senator's name, were very unpleasant experiences. Following the summer my feeling of emptiness was still there, the questions about myself, my purpose, what my life was all about. The doubts that had invaded my consciousness last February hung over me like a shroud.

The meeting in March with Phillips, meanwhile, had remained vivid in my memory. I recalled his warmth, his kindness, the serenity of his face, and the startling words, "I have accepted Jesus Christ and committed my life." I hadn't understood them, but they had a ring of simple, shameless sincerity. Tom represented everything that Watergate and Washington were not: decency, openness, truth. I thought often of Tom's words during this stormy time; even more often I recalled the expression on his face, something radiant, peaceful, and very real. I envied it, whatever it was. Finally, I decided to give Tom a call.

I arrived at Tom's home, and at his insistence, first the dark gray business-suit jacket, then my tie came off. He, fresh from playing tennis with his teenagers, pulled a wrought-iron ottoman close to the comfortable outdoor settee I sat on.

"Tell me, Chuck," he began, "are you okay?" It was the same question he had asked in March.

As the president's confidant and so-called big-shot Washington lawyer, I was still keeping my guard up. "I'm not doing too badly, I guess. All of this Watergate business, all the accusations—I suppose it's wearing me down some. But I'd rather talk about you, Tom. You've changed and I'd like to know what happened."

Tom drank from his glass of iced tea and sat back reflectively. Briefly he reviewed his past, the rapid rise to power at Raytheon: executive vice-president at thirty-seven, president when he was only forty. He had done it with hard work, day and night, nonstop.

"The success came, all right, but something was missing," he mused. "I felt a terrible emptiness. Sometimes I would get up in the middle of the night and pace the floor of my bedroom or stare out into the darkness for hours at a time."

"I don't understand it," I interrupted. "I knew you in those days, Tom. You were a straight arrow, had a good family life, were successful; in fact everything was going your way."

"All that may be true, Chuck, but my life wasn't complete. I would go to the office each day and do my job, striving all the time to make the company succeed, but there was a big hole in my life. I began to read the Scriptures, looking for answers. Something forced me to search, made me realize I needed a personal relationship with God."

MY NUMBER WAS UP

A prickly feeling ran down my spine. Maybe what I had gone through in the past several months wasn't so unusual after all—except I had not sought spiritual answers. I had not even been aware that finding a personal relationship with God was possible. I pressed him to explain the apparent contradiction between the emptiness inside while seeming to enjoy the affluent life.

"It may be hard to understand," Tom chuckled. "But I didn't seem to have anything that mattered. It was all on the surface. All the material things in life are meaningless if a man hasn't discovered what's underneath them. One night I was in New York on business and noticed that Billy Graham was having a Crusade in Madison Square Garden," Tom continued. "I went—curious, I guess—hoping maybe I'd find some answers. What Graham said that night put it all into place for me. I saw what was missing: the personal relationship with Jesus Christ, the fact that I hadn't ever asked Him into my life; I hadn't turned my life over to Him. So I did it—that very night at the Crusade."

Tom explained that after inviting Christ to come into his life that he could feel His presence and His peace. He also explained that accepting Christ simply meant asking. To me, Jesus had always been an historical figure, but Tom explained that you could hardly invite Him into your life if you didn't believe that He is alive today, that the Resurrection is a reality, and that His Spirit is a part of today's scene.

With any other man, the notion of relying on God would have seemed to me to be pure Pollyanna. Yet I had to be impressed with the way this man ran his company in the equally competitive world of business: ignoring his enemies, trying to follow God's ways and not the often cutthroat ethics of corporate business. And since his conversion Raytheon had never done better. Maybe there was something to it.

"Chuck, I don't think you will understand what I'm saying about God until you are willing to face yourself honestly and squarely. This is the first step." Tom reached to the corner table and picked up a small paperback book. I read the title: *Mere Christianity* by C. S. Lewis.

"I suggest you take this with you and read it while you are on vacation." Tom started to hand it to me, then paused. "Let me read you one chapter."

THE VICE OF PRIDE
I leaned back, still on the defensive, my mind and emotions whirling.

> There is one vice of which no man in the world is free; which every one in the world loathes when he sees it in someone else; and of which hardly any people, except Christians, ever imagine that they are guilty themselves. I have heard people admit that they are bad-tempered, or that they cannot keep their heads about girls or drink, or even that they are cowards. I do not think I have ever heard anyone who was not a Christian accuse himself of this vice. . . . There is no fault . . . which we are more unconscious of in ourselves. And the more we have it ourselves, the more we dislike it in others.
> The vice I am talking of is pride or self-conceit. . . . Pride leads to every

other vice: it is the complete anti-God state of mind.

As he read, I could feel a flush coming into my face and a curious burning sensation that made the night seem even warmer. Lewis's words seemed to pound straight at me.

. . . it is pride which has been the chief cause of misery in every nation and every family since the world began. Other vices may sometimes bring people together: you may find good fellowship and jokes and friendliness among drunken people or unchaste people. But pride always seems enmity—it is enmity. And not only enmity between man and man, but enmity to God.

In God you come up against something which is in every respect immeasurably superior to yourself. Unless you know God as that—and, therefore, know yourself as nothing in comparison—you do not know God at all. As long as you are proud you cannot know God. A proud man is always looking down on things and people: and, of course, as long as you are looking down, you cannot see something that is above you.

Suddenly I felt naked and unclean, my bravado defenses gone. I was exposed, unprotected, for Lewis's words were describing me. As he continued, one passage in particular seemed to sum up what had happened to all of us at the White House: "For pride is spiritual cancer: it eats up the very possibility of love, or contentment, or even common sense."

Tom finished the chapter on pride and shut the book.

That one chapter ripped through the protective armor in which I had unknowingly encased myself for forty-two years. I had never thought of anything being "immeasurably superior" to myself, or if I had in fleeting moments thought about the infinite power of God, I had not related Him to my life. In those brief moments while Tom read, I saw myself as I never had before. And the picture was ugly.

"How about it, Chuck?" Tom's question jarred me out of my trance. I knew precisely what he meant. Was I ready to make the same decision about Christ as he had made in New York?

"Tom, you've shaken me up. I'll admit that. But I can't tell you I'm ready to make the kind of commitment you did. I've got to be certain. I've got to learn a lot more, be sure all my reservations are satisfied. I've got a lot of intellectual hang-ups to get past."

Tom paused, then he smiled, saying, "I understand, I understand."

"You see," I continued, "I saw men turn to God in the Marine Corps; I did once myself. Then afterward it's all forgotten and everything is back to normal. Foxhole religion is just a way of using God. How can I make a commitment now? My whole world is crashing down around me. How can I be sure I'm not just running for shelter and that when the crisis is over I'll forget it? I've got to answer all the intellectual arguments first, and if I can do that, I'll be sure."

"I understand," Tom repeated quietly.

A DAM BREAKS

We then headed for the door, Tom stopped to pray for me before I left. By the time I got to my car I was crying, mad at myself for feeling weak. As I drove out of Tom's driveway, the tears were flowing uncontrollably. I pulled off to the side of the road not a block from Tom's house. I forgot about machismo, about pretenses, about fears of being weak. And as I did, I began to experience a wonderful feeling of being released.

Then came the strange sensation that water was not only running down my cheeks, but surging through my whole body as well, cleansing and cooling as it went. They weren't tears of sadness and remorse, nor of joy—but somehow, tears of relief. That night, not knowing what I was asking, I asked God for His help. There alone, in the quiet of the dark night,

I knew for the first time that I was no longer alone at all.

That week Patty and I took our vacation in a cottage in the lovely old fishing village of Boothbay Harbor along the New England coast. Patty wanted very much to relax and tune out the Watergate crisis for awhile. And I? I could hardly wait to get unpacked and dive into Lewis's book.

As I opened *Mere Christianity* I thought, *Perhaps Lewis approaches God on the intuitive, emotional level.* I did not know how wrong I was. Instead, I found myself face-to-face with an intellect so disciplined, so lucid, so relentlessly logical that I could only be grateful I had never faced him in a court of law. The central thesis of Lewis's book and the essence of Christianity is summed up in one mind-boggling sentence: "Jesus Christ is God." Not just part of God, or just sent by God, or just related to God. *He was* (and therefore, of course, *is*) God.

Over the course of the next few days I grappled and struggled with those words. I puzzled over both Lewis's book as well as my recent time at Tom's. I asked myself whether Christ could really change my life? What would it mean for my professional life if I accepted Christ? Was I sure that this was true? I questioned my motives. I wondered if I was not simply seeking a safe port in the storm, a temporary hiding place?

No, I knew the time had come for me: I could not sidestep the central question Lewis (or God) had placed squarely before me. Was I to accept without reservations Jesus Christ as Lord of my life? It was like a gate before me. There was no way to walk around it. I would step through, or I would remain outside. A "maybe" or an "I need more time" would be kidding myself.

NO MORE KIDDING MYSELF

And so early that Friday morning, while I sat alone staring at the sea I love, words I had not been certain I could understand or say fell naturally from my lips: "Lord Jesus, I believe You. I accept You. Please come into my life. I commit it to You."

With these few words that morning, while the briny sea churned, came a sureness of mind that matched the depth of feeling in my heart. There came something more: strength and serenity, a wonderful new assurance about life, a fresh perception of myself and the world around me. In the process, I felt old fears, tensions, and animosities draining away. I was coming alive to things I'd never seen before, as if God was filling the barren void I'd known for so many months, filling it to its brim with a whole new kind of awareness.

As a result of my conversion I began to

see the Watergate crisis in a whole new light—both its gravity and its scandal. I saw the pride and the abuse of power. The pride that Lewis had talked about in *Mere Christianity*—the pride that seeks power to the exclusion of what is right, the pride that thrives on power, the pride that is often so hard to see and to admit, the pride that is enmity with God, and the pride that eats away love and contentment; that pride had led to the Watergate debacle. I knew that it was pride that had kept me from God, and pride that had led me down the wrong path. A pride that God said, and I came to realize, is within every person. I saw that truth clearly manifested in Watergate.

I came to realize that I had to do not only what I thought was best for the country, but also what was right. In the past I had always believed the answer was the same for both—that what we thought was best for the country was right. Now I knew different. I realized that how I now perceived the latter was often at odds with how others perceived the former. I realized the moral compromises of Watergate were simply not justified for any reason, least of all to protect the country.

Thus, my commitment to Jesus Christ changed my heart and mind, giving me new peace and freedom, as well as a new perspective and worldview. And not only did I perceive the whole Watergate scandal differently—but as I reflected on the conspiracy and the brevity of the attempted cover-up, I realized that Watergate does indeed offer a compelling argument for the resurrection of Jesus Christ.

Let me explain.

THE LESSONS OF WATERGATE

Modern criticism of the historical truth of the Resurrection and Christianity boils down to three propositions:

- First, that the disciples were mistaken (i.e., they never saw the resurrected Christ); or
- Second, that the disciples knowingly perpetrated a myth (i.e., a lie) intended as a symbol; or
- Third, the eleven disciples conceived a "Passover plot"—spirited the body of Christ out of the tomb and disposed of it neatly—and to their dying breaths maintained conspiratorial silence.

Let's consider each.

The first is the shakiest. After all, a man being raised from the dead is a rather mind-boggling event—not the kind of thing people are likely to be vague or indecisive about. The Scriptures state very honestly that the disciples were so staggered by Jesus' reappearance that at least one demanded the tangible proof of fingering the wounds in His hands and side.

Jesus knew human nature, knew they needed physical evidence. Luke says, "He showed himself to these men and gave many convincing proofs that he was alive. He appeared to them over a period of forty days . . ." (Acts 1:3). The records of the event, written independently by various eyewitness reporters, belie the possibility that the disciples were mistaken.

But could it have been a myth? This second theory seems plausible at first since it was customary in the first century to convey religious truths through symbols. But this assumes that all the disciples understood that they were using a symbolic device. Even a cursory reading of the Gospels reveals not allegory or fable, but a straightforward, narrative account. Moreover, Paul, an intimate associate of the original disciples, shatters the myth theory altogether when he argues that if Jesus was not *actually* resurrected, Christianity is a hoax, a sham. Nothing in Paul's writings remotely suggests mythology.

The myth theory is as untenable as the mistake theory. So if one is to assail the historicity of the Resurrection and therefore the deity of Christ, one must conclude that there was a conspiracy—a cover-up if you will—by eleven men with the complicity of up to five hundred others (since that number of people are reported to have been eyewitnesses of the resurrected Christ).

To subscribe to this argument, one must also be ready to believe that each disciple was willing to be ostracized by friends and family, live in daily fear of death, endure prisons, live penniless and hungry, sacrifice family, be tortured without mercy, and ultimately die—all without ever once renouncing that Jesus had risen from the dead!

This is why the Watergate experience is so instructive for me. If John Dean and the rest of us were so panic-stricken, not by the prospect of beatings and execution, but by political disgrace and a possible prison term, one can only speculate about the emotions of the disciples. Unlike the men in the White House, the disciples were powerless people, abandoned by their leader, homeless in a conquered land. Yet they clung tenaciously to their enormously offensive story that their Leader had risen from His ignoble death and was alive—and was the Lord.

THE TRUE NATURE OF HUMANITY

The Watergate cover-up reveals, I think, the true nature of humanity. None of the memoirs suggest that anyone went to the prosecutor's office out of such noble notions as putting the Constitution above the president or bringing rascals to justice, or even moral indignation. Instead, the writings of those involved are consistent recitations of the frailty of man. Even political zealots at the pinnacle of power will save their own necks in the crunch, though it may be at the expense of the one they profess to serve so zealously.

Is it really likely, then, that a deliberate cover-up, a plot to perpetuate a lie about the Resurrection, could have survived the violent persecution of the apostles, the scrutiny of early church councils, the horrendous purge of the first-century believers who were cast by the thousands to the lions for refusing to renounce the lordship of Christ? Is it not probable that at least one of the apostles would have caved in and renounced Christ before being beheaded or stoned? Is it not likely that some "smoking gun" document might have been produced, exposing the "Passover plot?" Surely one of the conspirators would have made a deal with the authorities.

Blaise Pascal, the extraordinary mathematician, scientist, inventor, and logician of the seventeenth century, was convinced of the truth of Christ by examination of the historical record. In his classic, *Pensées*, Pascal wrote:

The hypothesis that the apostles were knaves is quite absurd. Follow it out to the end and imagine these twelve men meeting after Jesus' death and conspiring to say that He had risen from the dead. This means attacking all the

44

powers that be. The human heart is singularly susceptible to fickleness, to change, to promises, to bribery. One of them had only to deny his story under these inducements, or still more because of possible imprisonment, torture and death, and they would all have been lost.

As Pascal correctly observes, man in his normal state will renounce his beliefs just as readily as Peter renounced Jesus before the Resurrection. But as the same Peter discovered after the Resurrection, there is a power beyond man that causes him to forsake all. It is the power of the God who revealed Himself in the person of Jesus Christ.

TAKE IT FROM ME

Take it from one who was inside the Watergate web looking out, who saw firsthand how vulnerable a cover-up is: Nothing less than a witness as awesome as the resurrected Christ could have caused those men to maintain to their dying whispers that Jesus is alive and Lord.

This weight of evidence tells me the apostles were indeed telling the truth: Jesus did rise bodily from the grave; and He speaks today, as He did then, with the absolute authority of the all-powerful God.

C. S. Lewis

C. S. LEWIS was born November 29, 1898, in Belfast, Ireland. He authored over thirty books, including the popular children's fantasy stories, the Chronicles of Narnia, as well as adult science fiction, literary criticism, poetry, and Christian apologetics, among these The Problem of Pain, The Screwtape Letters, The Great Divorce, Miracles, and The Four Loves. Lewis had served on the faculty of Magdalen College at Oxford University for almost thirty years when, in 1954, he accepted the professorship of medieval and Renaissance literature at Magdalen College, Cambridge University. Lewis served on the faculty there until a few months before his death on November 22, 1963, the same day that Aldous Huxley and John F. Kennedy died.

"Logic!" said the Professor half to himself. "Why don't they teach logic at these schools? There are only three possibilities. Either your sister is telling lies, or she is mad, or she is telling the truth."[1]

During the middle 1920s, Clive Staples Lewis began his career as a young Oxford don teaching English and philosophy at Magdalen College, Oxford. His was a sought-after position in those days. Fellowships were hard to come by after the war years, with a greater number of men vying for positions. These were men who had put off university, as Lewis had done after only one term, in order to fight in World War I.

Following the war, after serving his tour as a lieutenant in the army, Lewis returned to Oxford to continue his studies. Thoroughly at home at Oxford, Lewis relished getting back into academic life. It was during this time that Lewis began his quest in earnest for what he called "joy"—

a quest that was to lead him where he did not want to go.

A SCHOLAR OF DISTINCTION

Lewis began his schooling at Oxford bent on the profession of teaching after the completion of his studies. Academic life was what Lewis felt himself to be uniquely qualified and best suited for. He also enjoyed writing and poetry, even having a volume of poetry published upon his return to the university. But that interest in poetry had to be curtailed as Lewis began to read (what we would call "majoring in") both philosophy and classics at Oxford.

By the time of his final examinations, Lewis had taken a "first" in Mods (Greek and Latin literature) and a first in Greats (classics and philosophy). One first would have been an achievement of distinction, but two was outstanding.

But at that time Lewis decided to continue his education rather than try to obtain a teaching appointment right away. He knew his possibility for a position would be greatly enhanced if he could do well in a subject that would complement his excellent background in the classics and philosophy. With this in mind, he chose to read English and soon had taken another "first," namely, first class honors in the Honor School of English Language and Literature. He also won the Chancellor's Prize for an English essay he had written. This achievement is roughly equivalent in America to that of graduating summa cum laude with a triple major in classics, philosophy, and English literature.

During his study of English literature, Lewis found himself with a growing interest in Christianity, an interest that had been rekindled both by his friends and by literature. Rekindled, because though raised in a Christian home, Lewis early became a staunch atheist.

THE FORMATION OF A
YOUNG ATHEIST

Lewis's early life was a happy one, one he remembered with gratitude. He recalled it later as a time of "good parents, good food, and a garden (which then seemed large) to play in."[2]

However, when Jack (a nickname he carried with him from his childhood) was nine years old, his mother died and things took a turn for the worse. Shortly after her death, Lewis's father sent him and his brother Warren off to boarding school in England.

It was during this time that Lewis gave up the faith he had adopted from his parents as a boy. He began to view religion as esoteric and eventually gave it up with "the greatest relief."[3]

Lewis describes this period in his life as one of loss—a loss of faith, of virtue, and of simplicity (the simplicity of youth).

Ironically, it was also during this time of rejecting religion that Lewis began his quest for joy. The joy that he had once briefly experienced as a child began to return to him at this time in his life, an experience that was to be central throughout his career.

This return of joy was brought on, for the most part, by the beauty and majesty of mythology, especially Norse mythology, and all the worlds and possibilities that it created. It triggered within Lewis his romantic passion of life and of the heroic quest. (Norse mythology was an interest that would eventually help lead him to his close friend J. R. R. Tolkien, who also shared this interest.)

PURSUING THE ECHO OF JOY

Through these stories Lewis, a great lover of language and literature, would often experience the joy that had become the "supreme object of desire." Lewis described his first encounters with this joy as a child in his autobiography, *Surprised by Joy*.

The first was a memory of a memory. He recalled a time when his brother brought his toy garden into the house. A sensation of enormous bliss came over him and with it a desire—but for what he was not sure. He knew it was not just desire for a little toy garden. But somehow it had hinted at some far-off time or place for which he longed.

The second was a time in his childhood when, in reading Beatrix Potter's *Squirrel Nutkin*, he became so enamored with the idea of autumn that he could hardly contain himself. Again and again he would return to the book to have that otherworldly desire reawakened within him.

The third experience he recalled came through poetry, while reading Longfellow's *Saga of King Olaf*. In reading one brief refrain, "Balder the beautiful is dead, is dead," Lewis grasped for one brief instant a glimpse of something so intense that it defied description, except that it was "cold, spacious, severe, pale, and remote."

Of these early experiences Lewis recounts:

> The reader who finds these three episodes of no interest need read this book no further, for in a sense the central story of my life is about nothing else. For those who are still disposed to proceed, I will only underline the quality common to the three experiences; it is that of an unsatisfied desire which is itself more desirable than any other satisfaction. I call it joy, which is here a

technical term and must be sharply distinguished both from happiness and from pleasure. Joy (in my sense) has indeed one characteristic, and one only, in common with them; the fact that anyone who has experienced it will want it again.

Apart from that, and considered only in its quality, it might almost equally well be called a particular kind of unhappiness or grief. But then it is a kind we want. I doubt whether anyone who has tasted it would ever, if both were in his power, exchange it for all the pleasures in the world. But then joy is never in our power and pleasure often is.[4]

In small but rewarding ways the beauty and majesty, the other worlds and possibilities of mythology triggered within Lewis an echo of those childhood glimpses of joy, so much so that the reading and nature of myth helped him through some difficult times at boarding school. However, even Lewis's world of myth, which gave him such delight, also began to cause difficulties for him as his devotion to the subject continued to grow.

REALISM AND MYTH COLLIDE

Lewis found that his world of poetry and myth collided with his world of rationalism. On one side stood his imagination, on the other his intellect. Almost all that Lewis loved, he believed to be imaginary.

Almost all that he believed to be real was for him grim and meaningless. The only exceptions were his close friends and nature itself.

But even nature posed troubles for Lewis, who at that time was a thoroughgoing materialist and realist. It was puzzling to Lewis that nature at the same time could be both beautiful as well as cruel and wasteful. Rationalism offered no real joy or solace to him, but it did do one thing—it eliminated God and gave man a free hand. For this Lewis was grateful. He cherished his freedom, or what he believed to be his freedom, rather than what Christianity might hold. The horror of the Christian universe for him was that there was no exit, no way of escape; it was all boundaries, or so he thought.

Lewis had a deep-seated hatred of authority and of anyone who attempted to interfere with his life. At that time in his life, the Christian God simply represented a transcendent interferer, someone Lewis believed he was better off without.

With Lewis's passionate rejection of religion, it is a wonder that he did not become an outspoken critic of faith and belief. Lewis himself writes in his autobiography:

> Looking back on my life now, I am astonished that I did not progress into the opposite orthodoxy—did not become a leftist, atheist, satiric intellectual

of the type we all know so well. All the conditions seem to be present. I had hated my public school. I hated whatever I knew or imagined of the British Empire. And though I took very little notice of Morris's socialism (there were too many things in him interested me far more), continual reading of Shaw had brought it about that such embryonic political opinions as I had were vaguely socialistic. Ruskin had helped me in the same direction.

My lifelong fear of sentimentalism ought to have qualified me to become a vigorous "debunker." . . . I suppose that my Romanticism was destined to divide me from the orthodox intellectuals as soon as I met them; and also that a mind so little sanguine as mine about the future and about common action could only with great difficulty be made revolutionary.

Such, then, was my position: to care for almost nothing but the gods and heroes, the garden of the Hesperides, Lancelot, and the Grail, and to believe in nothing but atoms and evolution and military service. At times the strain was severe, but I think this was a wholesome severity.[5]

LOVE OF LEARNING

To prepare him for university, his father took Lewis out of boarding school, which was on the whole an unpleasant experience, and set him under a private tutor, W. T. Kirkpatrick, who was affectionately known to Lewis as "the Great Knock." Under Kirkpatrick, Lewis flourished. His love for learning soared to new heights. He could not get enough, especially of literature. Kirkpatrick taught Lewis to think, criticize and analyze, and to write logically. Although Lewis's atheism was greatly strengthened under Kirkpatrick, he owed a tremendous debt to him. Lewis acknowledges his great debt, writing in his autobiography years later that "my reverence [of him] to this day is undiminished."[6]

Also during this period in his life, Lewis began a correspondence with his Irish boyhood friend, Arthur Greeves, which would last until Lewis's death. Greeves, who was a Christian, never ceased praying for his friend, nor encouraging him in the many letters they wrote over the years.

It was during this time that Greeves asked Lewis what he thought of religion. Lewis replied that it was fine, provided you were not an educated or a thinking person. Greeves patiently listened, trying to ask questions that would provoke Lewis's thinking or help him to see the inconsistencies or consequences of his reasoning.

One time Greeves asked Lewis why with such a depressing outlook he did not simply commit suicide. To this Lewis answered that even with discouraging surroundings, he was having a good time and saw no reason not to enjoy life. He did not believe, however, that his atheism absolved him of moral responsibility. He believed the basis for moral action lay in the dignity of man. Years later Lewis showed the fallacy of that very reasoning in his BBC radio addresses and eventually in his book *Mere Christianity*.

Writing to Greeves served as a sounding board for Lewis. Their dialogue helped him to frame and shape his own changing beliefs. Later, it was to Arthur Greeves that Lewis first acknowledged that his atheism may not be as rock solid as he believed. Although he was unaware of it at the time, his atheism was beginning to show cracks in the dike. Even as Lewis continued his preparation for Oxford under Kirkpatrick and continued to read and read, the joy became rarer and rarer.

UNLOCKING NEW IDEAS

Not long before he was to enter Oxford, Lewis picked up *Phantastes* by George MacDonald, which, along with other of MacDonald's works, was to have a profound impact on Lewis's thinking. Here again, literature unlocked new ideas for him. Although he did not realize it at the time, *Phantastes* opened to Lewis a whole new side of Romanticism, a side associated with goodness, a side Lewis would eventually realize as holiness. These works by MacDonald brought Lewis a fresh glimpse of joy. And after reading *Phantastes*, Lewis realized that he had "crossed a great frontier" and remarked that he did not have "the faintest notion" what he had let himself in for in buying it.

Another author who was to have a dramatic impact on Lewis was G. K. Chesterton. Chesterton, like MacDonald, was a Christian, and his writings had a similar effect on Lewis. Lewis commented in his biography that he liked Chesterton for his "goodness." Not that this brought out any inclination for Lewis to be good; he was rather enjoying vice to the exclusion of virtue at the time. But he did appreciate the quality of goodness even though he saw no reason to emulate it. Of Chesterton and MacDonald he later stated,

In reading Chesterton, as in reading MacDonald, I did not know what I was letting myself in for. A young man who wishes to remain a sound atheist cannot be too careful of his reading. There are traps everywhere—"Bibles laid open, millions of surprises," as Herbert says, "fine nets and stratagems." God is, if I may say it, very unscrupulous.[7]

"NO MORE ROMANTIC DELUSIONS!"

However, upon entering Oxford after the war, Lewis determined to adopt a new outlook on life, an intellectual one that gave no quarter to sagas and romance literature or the likes of Chesterton and MacDonald. As Lewis tells it:

> There was to be no more pessimism, no more self-pity, no flirtations with any idea of the supernatural, no romantic delusions. In a word, like the heroine of Northanger Abbey, I formed the resolution "of always judging and acting in future with the greatest good sense." And good sense meant, for me at the moment, a retreat, almost a panic-stricken flight, from all the sort of Romanticism which had hitherto been the chief concern of my life.[8]

This new perspective satisfied Lewis for a time while things were going well. But then "the sky changed" and anxiety began to creep into Lewis's seemingly intellectual stronghold.[9]

First, two of his closest friends at Oxford, A. C. Harwood and Owen Barfield, had become theists. For Lewis, this was quite disturbing.

Second, Barfield's turn to theism—and eventually Christianity—created a "great war" between Lewis and his close friend.

This war led Lewis to abandon forever two elements of his own thought. The first element to be jettisoned was what Lewis called "my chronological snobbery."[10]

This view held that the intelligent thing to do was to uncritically accept the intellectual climate of your day under the assumption that whatever has gone out of date was, *ipso facto*, discredited. Lewis came to realize that for a view to be refuted, it must first be discredited. And if it was not refuted, the fact that it had gone out of fashion did not discredit it. A view's going out of fashion said nothing of its truth or falsity. With Kirkpatrick's strong emphasis on discovering truth inculcated from the past, this view was more palatable than the next one Lewis was forced to adopt.

Barfield argued that Lewis's realism— the view that what could be known is only knowable through the senses—was an untenable position. Barfield maintained that if moral judgments, abstract thoughts, and aesthetic experiences have any value or can lead to truth, then realism must be abandoned.

This Lewis did, adopting absolute idealism in its place. Lewis felt realism had to be abandoned because if a person believed only what he saw, then those things that he could not see, such as thoughts or values, would not exist. Lewis explained his idealism in the following words: "the whole universe was, in the last resort, mental; that our logic was participation in a cosmic *Logos*."[11]

ASCENDANT IDEALISM

Lewis's idealism, although impersonal, was absolute, perhaps even Absolute—a sort of "watered-down Hegelianism," as Lewis called it. But there was no belief in God here or the faith that went with it. However, here was a step toward theism, and a step toward Christianity, even though Lewis did not see that as yet. So, in one fell swoop, Lewis jettisoned both his realism and his materialism (the view that only the physical world exists) and accepted the idea that the unseen did exist. The dike was beginning to crumble.

In fact, by the time Lewis had finished the Greats at Oxford and entered his program in English literature, his interest in Christianity had been revived through the reading of English medieval literature—the literature that would eventually take him to a chair at Cambridge University. It was soon after his "first" in English that he took a number of temporary teaching posts at Oxford until he was elected to a fellowship at Magdalen College, Oxford. An ad in *The Times* announcing the appointment ran as follows:

The President and Fellows of Magdalen College have elected to an official Fellowship in the College as Tutor in English Language and Literature, for five years as from next June 25, Mr. Clive Staples Lewis, M.A. (University College). [A Tutor might be understood best in America as an assistant professor, and as the fellowship is renewed, an associate professor.][12]

THOUGHT-PROVOKING FRIENDS

Along with the election to his fellowship came new friendships into Lewis's life. Two of these were J. R. R. Tolkien (author of *The Lord of the Rings* trilogy) and H. V. V. "Hugo" Dyson. They became Lewis's life-long friends, and, as Christians, they played an important role in his coming to faith.

These new friends and the pleasure of finally settling into his chosen profession gave Lewis much enjoyment in his early years at Magdalen College. He particularly cherished the beautiful surroundings where his rooms overlooked a spectacular grove of trees and beautiful deer park.

Lewis's heavy work load kept him busy his first years as a tutor. This limited both his social activity and his writing. He tutored not only students from his own college, Magdalen, but also, during at least one term a year, a group of women from another college, that of Lady Margaret Hall.

During those early years, however, writing was not completely neglected. Lewis was still very interested in poetry. In his first year as tutor, he saw his allegorical poem *Dymer* completed and published.

The reviews were very favorable. As one reviewer wrote in the *Sunday Times*, "[Lewis's] long allegorical poem *Dymer* is executed with a consistent craftsmanship which excites admiration even where criticism is readiest to speak."[13]

HOUNDED BY HIS "ADVERSARY"
Even with all this success coming his way—that of his fellowship, the company of good friends and colleagues (something which Lewis dearly loved), and the success of his writing career—Lewis was a man of uneasy spirit. As Lewis tells it, the time had come for his "Adversary [as he was wont to speak of the God he had so earnestly sought to avoid] to make His final moves."[14]

Lewis called them "moves" because his life seemed like a chess match in which his pieces were spread all over the board in the most disadvantageous positions. The board was set for a checkmate, with the moves of his Adversary slowly pushing Lewis into an unsettling position.

The first move was the destruction of the last vestiges of the new outlook he had adopted upon entering Oxford. Lewis, after rereading a favorite classic, came to a turning point and realized he could no longer abandon his interest in the classics, sagas, and romantic heroic quests when they surfaced within him that intense longing for joy, or for that great unknown (unknown because he was still not sure what it was he was longing for). He was forever hooked.

The second move was a pivotal one. Shortly after reading Samuel Alexander's *Space, Time, and Deity*, Lewis realized that there was a distinction between "enjoyment" and "contemplation." For Alexander this meant a difference between "enjoying," say, the act of thinking or seeing, and "contemplating" what you are thinking about or seeing. Lewis adopted this distinction and realized it had greater consequences:

> I accepted this distinction at once and have ever since regarded it as an indispensable tool of thought. A moment later its consequences—for me quite catastrophic—began to appear. It seemed to me self-evident that one essential property of love, hate, hope, or desire was attention to their object. . . . You cannot hope and also think about hoping at the same moment; for in hope we look to hope's object and we interrupt this by (so to speak) turning round to look at the hope itself. Of course the two activities can and do alternate with great rapidity; but they are distinct and incompatible.[15]

In other words, there is a distinct difference between, say, the "experience of joy" and "thinking on that experience."

There is a difference between hope and thinking about hope. There is a difference between the one you love and thinking about the love itself.

Lewis saw that you could not do both at the same time. You either turn inward and thus focus on the experience—in which case you then eclipse the object that brought about the experience in the first place—or you concentrate on the very object that elicits that experience. What Lewis came to understand was that even joy was not an end in itself. He had been longing for the experience of joy, not realizing that it must be pointing to something else. The very attempt to turn inward to contemplate the experience of joy cut him off from its source. For Lewis, this newfound understanding as it applied to joy was an important turning point:

> This discovery flashed a new light back on my whole life. I saw that all my waiting and watching for joy, all my vain hopes to find some mental content on which I could, so to speak, lay my finger and say, "This is it," had been a futile attempt to contemplate the enjoyed. All that such watching and waiting ever *could* find would be either an image (Asgard, the Western Garden, or what not) or a quiver in the diaphragm. I should never have to bother again about these images or sensations.
>
> I knew now that they were merely the mental track left by the passage of

joy—not the wave but the wave's imprint on the sand. The inherent dialectic of desire itself had in a way already shown me this; for all images and sensations, if idolatrously mistaken for joy itself, soon honestly confessed themselves inadequate. All said, in the last resort, "It is not I. I am only a reminder. Look! Look! What do I remind you of?"[16]

Even with this discovery, Lewis did not yet see any particular way that it pointed to God. In looking back on that time, Lewis found it surprising that he could have overlooked what seemed so obvious in hindsight. But this new distinction, even when coupled with his idealism, still did not open a window to God. This was to come next.

A TURN TOWARD THEISM

The turn toward theism came in the next two moves, moves that were closely related. First, Lewis realized that he must begin to take his philosophy seriously. This was the result of linking his previous conclusions about joy to his idealistic philosophy. Lewis now knew that this joy was real, not just a "quiver in the diaphragm," and that it had found its source in his Absolute.

Second, Lewis had never really defined what he meant by his Absolute. And now that he had begun to teach philosophy as well as English, the need to clearly delineate his own philosophy to his students again forced him to take his philosophy seriously.

The result was that he had no idea what an absolute idealism was, and Hegel and other philosophers offered no help. At this point he made a shift to Berkeley's "God."

George Berkeley was a seventeenth century British idealistic philosopher who firmly believed in God. Lewis felt that he was being forced away from his absolute idealism because he could not draw any clear conclusions about what it meant. So he was drawn toward an idealism that made more sense, namely, Berkeley's. Here, at least, a form of God had entered the picture. Of that shift Lewis wrote:

> A tutor must make things clear. Now the Absolute cannot be made clear. Do you mean Nobody-knows-what, or do you mean a superhuman mind and therefore (we may as well admit) a Person? After all, did Hegel and Bradley [F. H.] and all the rest of them ever do more than add mystifications to the simple, workable, theistic idealism of Berkeley? I thought not. And didn't Berkeley's "God" do all the same work as the Absolute, with the added advantage that we had at least some notion of what we meant by Him? I thought He did.[17]

Lewis had become a quasi-theist. He

was not willing to completely accept Berkeley's God. Lewis rejected the notion of a personal God at this point and, rather than calling Him "God," preferred to call Him "Spirit," writing that "one fights for one's remaining comforts."[18]

The final move came shortly after Lewis read G. K. Chesterton's *The Everlasting Man*, from which he, for the first time, saw the whole Christian outline of history in a way that made sense. Although, as disturbing as that was to Lewis, it was not nearly as disturbing as the discovery he made when he entertained a man Lewis considered the hardest-boiled atheist he'd ever known (a man whose name Lewis does not reveal in his autobiography).

Seated across from Lewis in his room, on the other side of the fire, this atheist crushed Lewis when he remarked what good evidence there seemed to be for the historicity of the Gospels. He commented to Lewis, "Rum thing. All that stuff of Frazer's about the Dying God. Rum thing. It almost looks as if it had really happened once." Lewis's reaction was one of astonishment and discouragement:

To understand the shattering impact of it, you would need to know the man (who has certainly never since shown any interest in Christianity). If he, the cynic of cynics, the toughest of toughs, were not—as I would still have put it—

67

"safe," where could I turn? Was there no escape?[19]

Now God was closing in on Lewis. He gradually became aware that God was offering him a free choice, a choice that for Lewis was strangely unemotional. He felt moved by neither desires nor fears. He knew the choice was his, to open the door a crack and consider God's existence.

THE RELUCTANT CONVERT
This he finally did, and in doing so realized that he was surrounded by theists. For Lewis, nearly everyone was now in the "pack," including Plato, Dante, Mac-Donald, Herbert, Barfield, Tolkien, Dyson, and "joy" itself. The metaphor Lewis used was of a pack of hounds who were now chasing him, "the fox," who, "had been dislodged from the Hegelian Wood" [i.e., Lewis had been chased away from Hegel's inscrutable absolute spirit, which made no sense, toward God].[20]

He continued to wrestle with his own philosophy, ultimately coming to understand that idealism cannot be lived, that its spirit is not personal. An impersonal spirit cannot be prayed to.

Lewis now realized that his Adversary was not some impersonal spirit; rather, He was claiming, "I am the Lord"; "I am that I am"; "I am." Of that revelation Lewis wrote,

People who are naturally religious find difficulty in understanding the horror of such a revelation. Amiable agnostics will talk cheerfully about "man's search for God." To me, as I then was, they might as well have talked about the mouse's search for the cat.[21]

That response was a reflection of Lewis's lifelong concern not to be interfered with, of the fact that he wanted to call his soul his own. Yet as he clung to his freedom, God closed in on him. Here, taken from his autobiography, *Surprised by Joy*, he recounts how it happened.

You must picture me alone in that room in Magdalen, night after night, feeling, whenever my mind lifted even for a second from my work, the steady, unrelenting approach of Him whom I so earnestly desired not to meet. That which I greatly feared had at last come upon me. In the Trinity Term of 1929 I gave in, and admitted that God was God, and knelt and prayed: perhaps, that night, the most dejected and reluctant convert in all England. I did not then see what is now the most shining and obvious thing; the Divine humility which will accept a convert even on such terms. The Prodigal Son at least walked home on his own feet. But who can but duly adore that Love which will open the high gates to a prodigal who is brought in kicking, struggling, resentful, and darting his eyes in every direction for a chance of escape? The words *compelle intrare*, compel them to come in, have been so abused by wicked men that we shudder at them; but, properly understood, they plumb the depth of the Divine mercy. The hardness of God is kinder than the softness of men, and His compulsion is our liberation.[22]

IS CHRISTIANITY THE ONLY WAY?

Lewis's *conversion*, as he called it, was only to theism and not to Christianity. At this stage, he knew very little about the Incarnation or of a future life. The God to whom Lewis had yielded was utterly nonhuman, though He was personal. It had been a difficult surrender for Lewis to admit God's existence, to no longer keep Him at bay. The question now before him was one of understanding; namely, to understand more of God and what was true of Him.

Shortly after his conversion, Lewis began to attend church on Sundays and his college chapel on weekdays. Lewis did this not out of any special devotion to the church; he simply believed that a person should publicly acknowledge his decisions in some way. He simply chose church because he did not believe at the time it made much difference where he went. In fact, Lewis was not in the least ecclesiastical. The public aspect of church-going was not something he relished.

However, one practical result of this was that Lewis began reading the Gospel of John in Greek. This began a practice of daily Bible reading that Lewis continued for the rest of his life. Through reading the Gospels, Lewis began to get a more rounded picture of Christ and Christianity.

Lewis began to debate and argue Christianity with his closer friends, such as Tolkien, Barfield, and Dyson. But he said very little of his change to friends of his undergraduate days with the exception of A. K. Hamilton Jenkin and his lifelong friend, Arthur Greeves. To them he said he was not precisely "Christian," though he admitted by then that he might yet become one. Instead, he said that whereas once he would have said, "Shall I adopt Christianity?" he was at a point of waiting to see whether it would adopt him. That is, he had recognized that he wasn't the only party in the affair as he had once supposed himself to be.

In a letter to Arthur Greeves, with whom he kept up a steady correspondence, he wrote of a time with his brother, Warren, who was also his close friend and was at that time an officer in the army at home on leave. He said that Warren

. . . has been with us all the month here. . . . He and I even went together to Church twice: and—will you believe it— he said to me in conversation that he was beginning to think the religious view of things was after all true. Mind you (like me, at first), he didn't want it to be, nor like it: but his intellect is beginning to revolt from the semi-scientific assumptions we all grew up in, and the other explanation of the world seems to him daily more probable.[23]

THE TASTE OF TRUTH, NOT MYTH

Those letters are indicative of the change that had been slowly taking place in Lewis's thinking. Lewis had considered other religions besides Christianity as the possible expression of theism. But after sorting out what he called the perplexing multiplicity of religions, he concluded that there were only two possible answers: Hinduism or Christianity. Of these two Lewis further stated:

Everything else was either a preparation for, or else . . . a *vulgarization* of, these. Whatever you could find elsewhere you could find better in one of these. But Hinduism seemed to have two disqualifications. For one thing, it appeared to be not so much a moralized and philosophical maturity of paganism as a mere oil-and-water coexistence of philosophy side by side with paganism unpurged; the Brahmin meditating in the forest, and, in the village a few miles away, temple prostitution, *sati*, cruelty, monstrosity.

And secondly, there was no such historical claim as in Christianity. I was by now too experienced in literary criticism to regard the Gospels as myths. They had not the mythical taste. And yet the very matter which they set down in their artless, historical fashion—those narrow, unattractive Jews, too blind to the mythical wealth of the pagan world around them—was precisely the matter of the great myths. If ever a myth had become fact, had been incarnated, it would be just like this. And nothing else in all literature was just like this. Myths were like it in one way. Histories were like it in another. But nothing was simply like it.

And no person was like the Person it depicted; as real, as recognizable (ten times more so than Eckermann's Goethe or Lockhart's Scott), yet also luminous, lit by a light from beyond the world, a god. But if a god—we are no longer polytheists—then not a god, but God. Here and here only in all time the myth must have become fact; the Word, flesh; God, Man.[24]

The final transition for Lewis was almost in place. As he approached his conclusion, a resistance toward Christianity sprang up, almost as strong as his previous resistance toward theism.

Finally one evening, Lewis chose to dine with Tolkien and Dyson at Magdalen. Myth and resurrection were fresh on his mind. As the evening's conversation wore on, Lewis began to more clearly understand both the nature and purpose of Christianity. After dinner they took a stroll up Addison's Walk toward Lewis's room where they stayed and talked until 3:00 A.M., when Tolkien had to leave. Walking around the grounds at Oxford, Lewis and Dyson continued their conversation for another hour.

FEARS FINALLY BURIED

Some eight days later, Lewis and his brother, Warren, took a trip to Whipsnade Zoo. Of that trip Lewis writes in his autobiography:

> When we set out I did not believe that Jesus Christ is the Son of God, and when we reached the zoo I did. Yet I had not exactly spent the journey in thought. Nor in great emotion. "Emotional" is perhaps the last word we can apply to some of the most important events. It was more like when a man, after long sleep, still lying motionless in bed, becomes aware that he is now awake.[25]

Just a few days afterward, Lewis closed out a longer letter to Arthur Greeves with the fresh news, "I have just passed on from believing in God to definitely believing in Christ—in Christianity. I will try to explain this another time. My long night talk with Dyson and Tolkien had a good deal to do with it."[26]

The long and difficult journey had finally ended for Lewis. His fears were finally dislodged and buried and his life forever changed. In the end, his coming to Christianity was not as dramatic as his conversion to God, but the results were just as final. For purpose had now entered Lewis's life in the form of knowing and obeying God. The fruit of this purpose was to be most noticeable in his future writing.

BEYOND JOY
But what had become of joy, that unknown that Lewis had so long been seeking? Upon his conversion to theism, Lewis wrote that he did not know if he would have to give up any desire he might have for it. He believed that for all he knew God might have called for the total rejection of what he called joy. Lewis had no idea at the time of any connection between God and joy, or that ultimately it was God who had truly been the source of all that he had called joy.

After becoming a Christian, Lewis said the subject lost nearly all interest for him, although the experience had not passed away. He wrote:

The old stab, the old bittersweet, has come to me as often and as sharply since my conversion as at any time of my life whatever. But I now know that the experience, considered as a state of my own mind, had never had the kind of importance I once gave it. It was valuable only as a pointer to something other and outer. While the other was in doubt, the pointer naturally loomed large in my thoughts. When we are lost in the woods, the sight of a signpost is a great matter. He who first sees it cries, "Look!" The whole party gathers round and stares. But when we have found the road and are passing signposts every few miles, we shall not stop and stare. They will encourage us and we shall be grateful to the authority that set them up.[27]

Lewis had, indeed, found the road and was about to begin a whole new journey— a journey that would eventually find its way to, and beyond, what Lewis liked to call "The Shadow-Lands" in *The Last Battle*, his final book of *The Chronicles of Narnia*. In this book, Lewis tells where this final journey will ultimately take him. A journey that really began as a quest for joy by a young atheist, who chose to follow the signposts along the way.

Aslan turned to them and said: ". . . you are—as you use to call it in the Shadow-Lands—dead. The term is over: the holidays have begun. The dream is ended: this is the morning."
. . . And for us this is the end of all

the stories, and we can most truly say that they all lived happily ever after. But for them it was only the beginning of the real story. All their life in this world and all their adventures in Narnia had only been the cover and the title page: now at last they were beginning Chapter One of the Great Story which no one on earth has read: which goes on for ever: in which every chapter is better than the one before.[28]

Josh McDowell

JOSH McDOWELL is one of the most popular speakers on the world scene today. In the last twenty-three years he has given more than eighteen thousand talks to over 8 million students and faculty at a thousand universities and high schools in seventy-two countries. Josh is author of thirty-two best-selling books and has been featured in twenty-seven films and videos and two TV specials.

Josh graduated cum laude from Kellogg College in economics and business. He finished graduate school magna cum laude with degrees in languages and theology. He is a member of two national honor societies and was selected by the Jaycees in 1976 as one of the "Outstanding Young Men in America." He holds honorary doctorate degrees in law and theology.

Thomas Aquinas wrote: "There is within every soul a thirst for happiness and meaning."

I wanted to be happy. There's nothing wrong with that. I also wanted to find meaning in life. I wanted answers to the questions: Who am I? Why in the world am I here? Where am I going?

More than that, I wanted to be free. Freedom to me was not going out and doing what I wanted to do. Freedom was having the power to do what I knew I ought to do . . . but didn't have the power to do.

So I started looking for answers. It seemed that almost everyone was into some sort of religion, so I did the obvious thing and took off for church.

I must have found the wrong church, though. Some of you know what I mean: I felt worse inside the church than I did outside.

I've always been very practical, and when one thing doesn't work, I chuck it.

So I chucked religion. The only thing I had ever gotten out of religion was the change I took out of the offering plate to buy a milkshake. And that's about all many people ever gain from "religion."

I began to wonder if prestige was the answer. So in college I ran for freshman class president and got elected. It was neat knowing everyone on campus, having everyone say, "Hi, Josh," making the decisions, spending the university's money and the students' money to get speakers I wanted. It was great, but it wore off like everything else I had tried.

I was like a boat out in the ocean being tossed back and forth by the waves, the circumstances. And I couldn't find anyone who could tell me how to live differently *or* give me the strength to do it.

Then I began to notice people who seemed to be riding above the circumstances of university life. One important thing I noticed was that they seemed to possess an inner, constant source of joy— a state of mind not dependent on their surroundings. They were disgustingly happy. They had something I didn't have . . . and I wanted it.

As I began purposely to spend more time with these people, we ended up sitting around a table in the student union one afternoon. Finally, I leaned back in my chair and said, "Tell me, have you always been this way, or has something changed your lives? Why are you so different from the other students, the leaders on campus, the professors? Why?"

One student looked me straight in the eye—with a little smile—and said two words I never thought I'd hear as part of any solution in a university. She said, "Jesus Christ."

I said, "Oh, for heaven's sake, don't give me that garbage. I'm fed up with religion; I'm fed up with the church. Don't give me that garbage about religion."

She shot back, "Mister, I didn't say 'religion,' I said, 'Jesus Christ.' "

It wasn't long before these new friends challenged me intellectually to examine the claims that Jesus Christ is God's Son, that He took on human flesh, that He lived among real men and women and died on the cross for the sins of mankind, that He was buried and He arose three days later and could change a person's life in the twentieth century.

At first I thought it was a joke. How ridiculous. It was my opinion that most Christians had two brains; one was lost and the other was out looking for it. Oh, I used to wait for a Christian student to speak up in class. I could tear him or her up one side and down the other side, even beating my professors to the punch. I knew answers to any argument a Christian could bring up. But these people kept challenging me over and over and over again.

Finally, I accepted their challenge. I did

it out of pride, to refute them. But I didn't know there were facts. I didn't know there was evidence that a person could evaluate. In fact, the background of my first book, *Evidence That Demands a Verdict*, was done to enable me to write a book that would make an intellectual joke of their kind of beliefs.

THE SEARCH CONTINUES

So I set out and spent a lot of money to make an intellectual joke of Christianity, but after two years it backfired on me. I came to the conclusion that Christ had to be who He claimed to be. "Now wait a minute," you say. "You came to that conclusion intellectually?"

That's right. Let me show you. I concluded that if I could show that either one of two basic areas was not historically trustworthy or true I had my case won against Christianity.

WHAT ABOUT THE NEW TESTAMENT?

The first area was if I could show that the New Testament was not historically reliable. I figured there was no question about that. It was written years later, I thought, and all those myths and legends had crept in, along with all kinds of other errors and discrepancies. That's all I had to do, but, as I said, it backfired.

When I speak in a literature or history class now I make the statement that I believe there's more evidence for the historical reliability of the New Testament than for any ten pieces of classical literature put together. Dr. F. F. Bruce of the University of Manchester in England puts it this way: "If the New Testament were a collection of secular writings, their authenticity would generally be regarded as beyond all doubt."[1]

For example, when you study history you need to develop a historiography, a proper approach to evaluating historical documents. There are three basic tests. One is the *bibliographical* test, another is the *internal evidence* test, and then the *external evidence* test.

Let me just touch on the bibliographical test, which asks questions about manuscripts. A manuscript is a handwritten copy rather than a printed one. One question this test asks is how many manuscripts you have. The more manuscripts you have, the easier it is to reconstruct the original (referred to as the *autograph*) and check out any errors or discrepancies.

Let me tell you what I found in relation to the New Testament. When I first came out with my *Evidence That Demands a Verdict* book in 1974, I was able to document 14,000 manuscripts of just the New Testament (that's not counting the Old Testament). Now, in the revised addition that's come out just recently, I've been able to document 24,633 manuscripts of just the New Testament. Do you know the Number Two book in all of history in manuscript authority? It's the *Iliad* by Homer, which has 643 manuscripts.

Dr. Clark Pinnock, Professor of Interpretations at McMasters University in Toronto, writes,

> There exists no document from the ancient world witnessed by so excellent a set of textual and historical testimonies, and offering so superb an array of historical data on which the intelligent decision may be made. An honest [person] cannot dismiss a source of this kind. Skepticism regarding the historical credentials of Christianity is based upon an irrational bias.[2]

WHAT ABOUT THE RESURRECTION?
The second area that I felt would be even simpler to discount was the Resurrection. Everything that Jesus Christ taught, lived, and died for was based on His Resurrection. All I had to do was show that the Resurrection never took place. That would be easy; I'd never met anyone who'd been resurrected. But that, too, backfired on me, and in fact led to

my writing *The Resurrection Factor* because of the evidence.

Have you heard of Dr. Simon Greenleaf, a man who held the Royal Professorship of Law at Harvard? He was a skeptic, often mocking the Christians in his ~classes. One day they got tired of that and challenged him to take the three volumes he had written on the laws of legal evidence and apply them to the Resurrection. After much persuasion he did that. In the process he became a Christian and went on to write a book that's now printed by Baker Book House. Greenleaf came to the conclusion that the resurrection of Jesus Christ is one of the best established events in history according to the laws of legal evidence.

Dr. E. M. Blaiklock, former Professor of Classics at Auckland University, concluded that

> I claim to be an historian. My approach to Classics is historical. And I tell you that the evidence for the life, the death, and the resurrection of Christ is better authenticated than most of the facts of ancient history. . . .

An Englishman, John Singleton Copley, better known as Lord Lyndhurst, is recognized as one of the greatest legal minds in British history. He was the solicitor-general of the British government, attorney-general of Great Britain, three times

High Chancellor of England, and elected as High Steward of the University of Cambridge, thus holding in one lifetime the highest offices ever conferred upon a judge in Great Britain.

Upon Copley's death, among his personal papers were found his comments concerning the Resurrection in the light of legal evidence and why he became a Christian: "I know pretty well what evidence is; and I tell you, such evidence as that for the Resurrection has never been broken down yet."[3]

Lord Chief Justice of England, Lord Darling, once said that "no intelligent jury in the world could fail to bring in a verdict that the resurrection story is true."[4]

As I delved further into my research on Christ, I discovered that men and women down through the ages have been divided over the question, "Who is Jesus?"

It didn't take long for the people who knew Jesus to realize that He was making astounding claims about Himself. Especially during the trial of Jesus—the trial that eventually led Him to the cross—I found one of the clearest references to Jesus' claims of deity.

Then the High Priest asked him, "Are you the Messiah, the Son of God?"

Jesus said, "I am, and you will see me sitting at the right hand of God, and returning to earth in the clouds of heaven." (Mark 14:61-62)

Jesus claimed to be God. He didn't leave any other option open. His claim must be either true or false. Jesus' question to His disciples, "Who do *you* think I am?" (Matthew 16:15) has several alternatives.

WAS HE A LIAR?

If, when Jesus made His claims, He knew that He was not God, then He was lying and deliberately deceiving His followers. And if He was a liar, then He was also a hypocrite because He told others to be honest, whatever the cost, while He Himself taught and lived a colossal lie.

This view of Jesus, however, doesn't coincide with what we know either of Him or the results of His life and teachings. Whenever Jesus has been proclaimed, lives have been changed for the good, nations have been changed for the better. Thieves have been made honest, alcoholics have been cured, hateful individuals have become channels of love, unjust persons have become just.

William Lecky, one of Great Britain's most noted historians and a dedicated opponent of organized Christianity, wrote about Jesus' ministry: "The simple record of these three short years of active life has done more to regenerate and soften mankind than all the discourses of philosophers and all the exhortations of moralists."[5]

Someone who lived as Jesus lived, taught as Jesus taught, and died as Jesus died could not have been a liar. What other alternatives are there?

WAS HE A LUNATIC?

If it is inconceivable for Jesus to be a liar, then couldn't He actually have thought Himself to be God, but been mistaken? After all, it's possible to be sincere and wrong.

Someone who believes he is God sounds like someone today believing himself to be Napoleon. He would be deluded and self-deceived, and probably would be locked up so he wouldn't hurt himself or anyone else. Yet in Jesus we don't observe the abnormalities and imbalance that usually go along with being deranged. His poise and composure when confronted by His enemies would certainly be amazing if He were insane.

Here is a man who spoke some of the most profound sayings ever recorded. His instructions have liberated many individuals in mental bondage.

A student at a California university told me that his psychology professor had said in class that "all he has to do is pick up the Bible and read portions of Christ's teachings to many of his patients. That's all the counseling they need."

Psychiatrist J. T. Fisher, speaking of

Jesus' popular "Sermon on the Mount" (Matthew 5–7), says this: "For nearly two thousand years the Christian world has been holding in its hands the complete answer to its restlessness and fruitless yearnings. Here . . . rests the blueprint for successful human life with optimism, mental health, and contentment."[6]

WAS HE LORD?

I cannot personally conclude that Jesus was a liar or a lunatic. The only other alternative is that He is the Christ—the Son of God—as He claimed to be.

When I discuss this with many people, it's interesting how they respond. I share with them the claims Jesus made about Himself and then the material about Jesus being a liar, lunatic, or Lord. When I ask if they believe Jesus was a liar, there is usually a sharp, "No!"

Then I ask, "Do you believe He was a lunatic?"

The reply is, "Of course not."

Then, "Do you believe He is God?"

But before I can get a breath in edgewise, there is a resounding, "Absolutely not."

Yet, one has only so many choices. One of these options must be true.

The issue with these three alternatives is not *Which is possible?* for it is obvious that any of the three could have been possible. But, rather the question: *Which is more probable?*

Who you decide Jesus Christ is must not be an idle intellectual exercise. You cannot put Him on the shelf while calling Him a great moral teacher. That is not a valid option, because if He was so great and moral, what are you going to do with His claim to be God?

If He was a liar or lunatic, then He can't qualify as a great moral teacher. And if He was a great moral teacher, then He is much more as well. He is either a liar, a lunatic, or the Lord God. I had to make a choice.

THE COMPELLING CONCLUSION
Finally, after gathering the evidence, I was compelled to conclude that my arguments against Christianity wouldn't stand up. Jesus Christ *is* exactly who He claimed to be, the Son of God.

At that time, though, I had quite a problem. My mind told me all this was true, but my will was pulling me in another direction. I discovered that becoming a Christian was rather ego-shattering. Jesus Christ made a direct challenge to my will to trust him. Let me paraphrase Him: "Look! I have been standing at the door and I am constantly knocking. If anyone hears me calling him and opens the door, I will come in" (Revelation 3:20). I didn't care if He did walk on water or turn water into wine. I didn't want any party pooper around. I couldn't think of a faster way to ruin a good time. So here was my mind telling me Christianity was true, and my will was somewhere else.

Every time I was around those enthusiastic Christians, the conflict would begin. If you've ever been around happy people when you're miserable, you understand how they can bug you. They would be so happy and I would be so miserable that I'd literally get up and run right out of the student union. It came to the point where I'd go to bed at ten at night and I wouldn't get to sleep until four in the morning. I knew I had to get it off my mind before I went out of my mind!

In my second year at the university— on December 19, 1959, at 8:30 P.M.—I became a Christian. That night I prayed four things to establish a relationship with the resurrected, living Christ which has since transformed my life.

First, I said, "Lord Jesus, thank you for dying on the cross for me." Second, I said, "I confess those things in my life that aren't pleasing to you and ask you to forgive me and cleanse me." (The Bible says, "Though your sins are like scarlet, they shall be as white as snow.") Third, I said, "Right now, in the best way I know how, I open the door of my heart and life and trust you as my Savior and Lord. Take over the control of my life. Change me from the inside out. Make me the type of person you created me to be." The last thing I prayed was, "Thank you for coming into my life by faith." It was a faith based not upon ignorance but upon evidence and facts of history and God's Word.

THE CONSEQUENCES
You've probably heard religious people talk about their "bolt of lightning." Well, nothing so dramatic happened to me, but in time there were some very observable changes.

Mental Peace. I had been a person who always had to be occupied. I had to be over at my girl's place or somewhere in a rap session. I'd walk across campus, and my mind would be a whirlwind of conflicts. I'd sit down and try to study or think, and I couldn't.

But in a few months after I made the decision to trust Christ, a kind of mental peace began to develop. Don't misunderstand, I'm not talking about the absence of conflict. What I found in this relationship with Jesus wasn't so much the absence of conflict as it was the ability to cope with it. I wouldn't trade this for anything in the world.

Control of Temper. Another area that started to change was my bad temper. I used to "blow my stack" if somebody just looked at me cross-eyed. I still have the scars from almost killing a man my first year in the university. My temper was such an integral part of me, I didn't consciously seek to change it.

Then one day after my decision to put my faith in Christ, I arrived at a crisis, only to find that my temper was gone!

Freedom from Resentment. I had a lot of hatred in my life. It wasn't something outwardly manifested, but there was a kind of inward grinding. I was ticked off with people, things, issues.

The one person I hated more than anyone else in the world was my father. I despised him. He was the town alcoholic. And if you're from a small town and one of your parents is an alcoholic, you know what I'm talking about.

Everybody knew. My friends would come to high school and make jokes about my father. They didn't think it bothered me. I was laughing on the outside, but let me tell you I was crying on the inside. I'd go out in the barn and find my mother lying in the manure behind the cows. She'd been knocked down by my father and couldn't get up.

About five months after I made my decision for Christ, love for my father—a love from God through Jesus Christ—inundated my life. It took that resentment and turned it upside down. It was so strong, I was able to look my father squarely in the eye and say, "Dad, I love you." I really meant it.

When I transferred to a private university, I was in a serious car accident. With my neck in traction, I was taken home. I'll never forget my father coming into my room and asking, "Son, how can you love a father like me?"

I said, "Dad, six months ago I despised you." Then I shared with him my conclusions about Jesus Christ and how He had changed me.

Forty-five minutes later one of the greatest thrills of my life occurred. Somebody in my own family, someone who knew me so well I couldn't pull the wool over his eyes, my own father, said to me, "Son, if God can do in my life what I've seen Him do in yours, then I want to give Him the opportunity."

Usually changes take place over several days, weeks, or even years. But my father was changed right before my eyes. It was as though somebody reached in and turned on a light bulb. I've never seen such a rapid change before or since. My father touched alcohol only once after that. He got it as far as his lips, and that was it. He didn't need it any more.

I've come to one conclusion: a relationship with Jesus Christ changes lives. You can ignore Him; you can mock or ridicule Christianity. It's your decision. And yet, when all else is said and done, we must face the fact that Peter pointed out: "Jesus [is] the Messiah . . . There is salvation in no one else! Under all heaven there is no other name for men to call upon to save them" (Acts 4:11-12).

If you ask Him to take control of your life, start watching your attitudes and actions—because the Christ of the New Testament is in the business of forgiving sin, removing guilt, changing lives, and building new relationships.

Most important of all, we can experience the power of the risen Christ in our life today.

- First, we can know the freedom of having our sins forgiven.
- Second, we can be assured of eternal life and our own resurrection from the grave.
- Third, we can be released from a meaningless and empty life and be transformed into a new creature in Jesus Christ.

WHERE DO YOU STAND?
What do you think of Christ?

When I was confronted with the overwhelming evidence for Christ's resurrection, I had to ask the logical question: "What difference does all this evidence make to me? What difference does it make whether or not I believe Christ rose again and died on the cross for my sins?"

The answer was put best by something Jesus said to a man who doubted—Thomas. He told him, "I am the Way—yes, and the Truth, and the Life. No one can get to the Father except by means of me" (John 14:6).

Considering the fact that Jesus offers forgiveness of sin and an eternal relationship with God, who would be so foolhardy as to reject Him? Christ is alive! He is living today.

You can trust God right now by faith through prayer. Prayer is talking with God. God knows your heart and is not so concerned with your words as He is with the attitude of your heart. If you have never trusted Christ, you can do so right now.

The Four Spiritual Laws[1]

Just as there are physical laws that govern the physical universe, so there are spiritual laws that govern your relationship with God.

LAW ONE

GOD LOVES YOU AND OFFERS A WONDERFUL PLAN FOR YOUR LIFE.

God's Love. "For God so loved the world, that He gave His only begotten Son, that whoever believes in Him should not perish, but have eternal life" (John 3:16, NASB).

God's Plan. Christ said, "I came that they might have life, and might have it abundantly" (that it might be full and meaningful) (John 10:10, NASB).

Why is it that most people are not experiencing the abundant life? Because ...

LAW TWO

MAN IS SINFUL AND SEPARATED FROM GOD, THUS, HE CANNOT KNOW AND EXPERIENCE GOD'S LOVE AND PLAN FOR HIS LIFE.

Man Is Sinful. "For all have sinned and fall short of the glory of God" (Romans 3:23, NASB).

Man was created to have fellowship with God; but, because of his own stubborn self-will, he chose to go his own independent way, and fellowship with God was broken. This self-will, characterized by an attitude of active rebellion or passive indifference, is an evidence of what the Bible calls sin.

Man Is Separated. "For the wages of sin is death" (spiritual separation from God) (Romans 6:23, NASB).

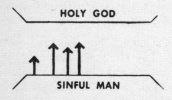

This diagram illustrates that God is holy and man is sinful. A great gulf separates the two. The arrows illustrate that man is continually trying to reach God and the abundant life through his own efforts, such as a good life, philosophy, or religion.

The Third Law explains the only way to bridge this gulf. . . .

LAW THREE

JESUS CHRIST IS GOD'S ONLY PROVISION FOR MAN'S SIN. THROUGH HIM YOU CAN KNOW AND EXPERIENCE GOD'S LOVE AND PLAN FOR YOUR LIFE.

He Died in Your Place. "But God demonstrates His own love toward us, in that while we were yet sinners, Christ died for us" (Romans 5:8, NASB).

He Rose from the Dead. "Christ died for our sins. . . . He was buried. . . . He was raised on the third day according to the Scriptures. . . . He appeared to [Peter], then to the twelve. After that He appeared to more than five hundred . . ." (1 Corinthians 15:3-6, NASB).

He Is the Only Way to God. "Jesus said to him, 'I am the way, and the truth, and the life; no one comes to the Father, but through Me'" (John 14:6, NASB).

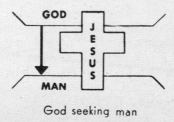

God seeking man

This diagram illustrates that God has bridged the gulf that separates us from Him by sending His Son, Jesus Christ, to die on the cross in our place to pay the penalty for our sins.

It is not enough to know these three laws nor even to give intellectual assent to them . . .

LAW FOUR

WE MUST INDIVIDUALLY RECEIVE JESUS CHRIST AS SAVIOR AND LORD; THEN WE CAN KNOW AND EXPERIENCE GOD'S LOVE AND PLAN FOR OUR LIVES.

We Must Receive Christ. "But as many as received Him, to them He gave the right to become children of God, even to those who believe in His name" (John 1:12, NASB).

We Receive Christ through Faith. "For by grace you have been saved through faith; and that not of yourselves, it is the gift of God; not as a result of works, that no one should boast" (Ephesians 2:8-9, NASB).

When we receive Christ, we experience a new birth. (Read John 3:1-8.)

We Receive Christ by Personal Invitation. (Christ is speaking) "Behold, I stand at the door and knock; if anyone hears My voice and opens the door, I will come in to him" (Revelation 3:20, NASB).

Receiving Christ involves turning to

God from self (repentance) and trusting Christ to come into our lives to forgive our sins and to make us the kind of people He wants us to be. Just to agree intellectually that Jesus Christ is the Son of God and that He died on the cross for our sins is not enough. Nor is it enough to have an emotional experience. We receive Jesus Christ by faith, as an act of the will.

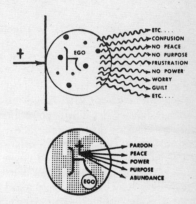

Which circle best represents your life?

Which circle would you like to have represent your life?

The following explains how you can receive Christ:

You Can Receive Christ Right Now by Faith through Prayer. (Prayer is talking with God.)

God knows your heart and is not so concerned with your words as He is with the attitude of your heart. The following is a suggested prayer.

> Lord Jesus, I need You. Thank You for dying on the cross for my sins. I open the door of my life and receive You as my Savior and Lord. Than You for forgiving my sins and giving me eternal life. Take control of the throne of my life. Make me the kind of person You want me to be.

Does this prayer express the desire of your heart?

If it does, pray this prayer right now, and Christ will come into your life, as He promised.

How to Know That Christ Is in Your Life. Did you receive Christ into your life? According to His promise in Revelation 3:20, where is Christ right now in relation to you? Christ said that He would come into your life. Would He mislead you? On what authority do you know that God has answered your prayer? (The trustworthiness of God Himself and His Word.)

The Bible Promises Eternal Life to All who Receive Christ. "And the witness is this, that God has given us eternal life, and this life is in His Son. He who has the Son has the life; he who does not have the Son of God does not have the life. These things I have written to you who believe in the name of the Son of God, in order that you may know that you have eternal life"

(1 John 5:11-13, NASB).

Thank God that Christ is in your life and that He will never leave you. (See Hebrews 13:5.) You can know on the basis of His promise that Christ lives in you and that you have eternal life, from the very moment you invite Him in. He will not deceive you.

Meet with Other Christians. The Christian life was not meant to be lived alone. God's Word admonishes us not to forsake "the assembling of ourselves together . . ." (Hebrews 10:25, NASB). Several logs burn brightly together; but put one aside on the cold hearth and the fire goes out. So it is with your relationship to other Christians. If you do not belong to a church, do not wait to be invited. Take the initiative; call the pastor of a nearby church where Christ is honored and His Word is preached. Start this week, and make plans to attend regularly.

Special Materials Are Available for Christian Growth. If you have established a relationship with God through Christ as you were reading the above, please write me and tell me about it. I would be delighted to send you some materials that will help you in your ongoing walk with God.

Josh McDowell
Box 1000
Dallas, TX 75221

Notes

CHAPTER 2

1. C. S. Lewis, *The Lion, the Witch, and the Wardrobe* (New York: Macmillian, 1950), 45.
2. C. S. Lewis, *Surprised by Joy* (Harcourt, Brace, and World, Inc., 1955), 5.
3. Ibid., 66.
4. Ibid., 17–18.
5. Ibid., 173–174.
6. Ibid., 148.
7. Ibid., 191.
8. Ibid., 201.
9. Ibid., 205.
10. Ibid., 207.
11. Ibid., 11.
12. Roger Lancelyn Green and Walter Hooper, *C. S. Lewis: A Biography* (New York: Harcourt Brace Jovanovich, 1974), 82.
13. Ibid., 89.
14. *Surprised*, 216.
15. Ibid., 218.
16. Ibid., 219–220.
17. Ibid., 222–223.
18. Ibid., 223.
19. Ibid., 224.
20. Ibid., 225.
21. Ibid., 227.
22. Ibid., 228–229.
23. C. S. Lewis, *The Letters of C. S. Lewis to Arthur Greeves*, ed. Walter Hooper (New York:

Collier/Macmillan, 1979), 401.

24. *Surprised,* 235–236.
25. Ibid., 237.
26. *Letters,* 425.
27. *Surprised,* 238.
28. C. S. Lewis, *The Last Battle* (New York:
    Collier/Macmillan, 1977, ©1956), 183–184.

CHAPTER 3
 1. Frederick F. Bruce, *The New Testament Documents:
    Are They Reliable?* 5th ed. (Downers Grove, Ill.,
    InterVarsity Press, 1960), 15.
 2. From personal correspondence with the author,
    1981.
 3. Wilbur Smith, *Therefore Stand* (Grand Rapids:
    Baker Book House, 1965), 425–584.
 4. Val Grieve, *Verdict on the Empty Tomb* (London:
    Church Pastoral Society, 1976), 26.
 5. William E. Lecky, *History of European Morals from
    Augustus to Charlemagnem,* Vol. 2 (New York:
    D. Appleton and Co., 1903), 8–9.
 6. J. T. Fisher and L. S. Hawley, *A Few Buttons
    Missing* (New York: The MacMillan Company,
    1947), 113.

SPECIAL FEATURE
 1. *The Four Spiritual Laws* is copyrighted material
    used by permission of Campus Crusade for
    Christ International, Arrowhead Springs, San
    Bernadino, CA 92403.

About the Author

JOSH McDOWELL is one of the most popular speakers on the world scene today. In the last twenty-three years he has given more than 18,000 talks to more than 8 million students and faculty at 1,000 universities and high schools in seventy-two countries. Josh is author of thirty-two best-selling books and has been featured in twenty-seven films and videos and two TV specials.

Josh graduated cum laude from Kellogg College in economics and business. He finished graduate school magna cum laude with degrees in languages and theology. He is a member of two national honor societies and was selected by the Jaycees in 1976 as one of the "Outstanding Young Men in America." He holds honorary doctorate degrees in law and theology.

Josh and his wife, Dottie, have four children and live in Julian, California.

POCKET GUIDES
FROM TYNDALE

• **The Best Way to Plan Your Day** by Edward Dayton and Ted Engstrom. With the guidelines in this book, you can learn to effectively set goals, determine priorities, and beat the time crunch. 72-0373-1

• **Christianity: Hoax or History?** by Josh McDowell. Was Jesus Christ a liar, a lunatic, or Lord? A popular speaker and author looks at the resurrection of Jesus and other claims of the Christian faith. 72-0367-7

• **Demons, Witches, and the Occult** by Josh McDowell and Don Stewart. Why are people fascinated with the occult? This informative guide will answer your questions about occult practices and their dangers. 72-0541-6

• **Facing Your Fears** by Norm Wright. A guide that gives specific help for those struggling with the fears of intimacy, failure, and losing control. 72-0825-3

• **Family Budgets That Work** by Larry Burkett. Customize a budget for your household with the help of this hands-on workbook. By the host of the radio talk show "How to Manage Your Money." 72-0829-6

• **Getting Out of Debt** by Howard L. Dayton, Jr. At last, a no-nonsense approach to your money problems. Here's advice on creating a budget, cutting corners, making investments, and paying off loans. 72-1004-5

• **Make Your Dream Come True** by Charles Swindoll. These ten inspirational chapters will lead any man or woman in the quest for inner strength and growth and help develop great character traits. 72-7007-2

• **The Perfect Way to Lose Weight** by Charles Kuntzleman and Daniel Runyon. Anyone can lose fat—and keep it off permanently. This tested program, developed by a leading physical fitness expert, shows how. 72-4935-9

POCKET GUIDES
FROM TYNDALE

• **Preparing for Childbirth** by Debra Evans. Expectant moms can replace their fears about childbirth with joyful anticipation. Includes suggestions for preparing for labor, breastfeeding, and more that will benefit both mothers and fathers. 72-4917-0

• **Raising Teenagers Right** by James Dobson. Dr. Dobson, an authority on child development, answers some of the most-asked questions about the teenage years: how to implement discipline, build confidence, and discuss puberty. 72-5139-6

• **Sex, Guilt & Forgiveness** by Josh McDowell. This book offers practical counsel on learning to forgive oneself and others following sexual experiences outside of marriage. 72-5908-7

• **Six Attitudes for Winners** by Norman Vincent Peale. Let an internationally known speaker and author help you replace fear, worry, apathy, and despair with courage, peace, hope, and enthusiasm. 72-5906-0

• **Skeptics Who Demanded a Verdict** by Josh McDowell. Three convincing stories of faith from some famous skeptics: C.S. Lewis, Charles Colson, and Josh McDowell. 72-5925-7

• **Temper Your Child's Tantrums** by James Dobson. You don't need to feel frustrated as a parent. The celebrated author and "Focus on the Family" radio host wants to give you the keys to firm, but loving, discipline in your home. 72-6994-5